BLOOD PERFUME

LOKANSHA BALYAN

Made with ♥ on the Notion Press Platform
www.notionpress.com

To- My permanent shelter, the one I love most; My mom

Contents

Contents

Preface

Vex my heart and hope to die,
    welcome to the bitter side. <3

BLOOD PERFUME

I had a fetish of fantasizing doom

Like a senseless sadist, born off the fumes

Pearls and prison and a witch on a broom

My happily ever after, when death consumes

Cannibal heart, a glamorized death cruise

Fell apart to save you like a melted fuse

Naivety caused art, but also the bruise

Risked it all, 'cause I had nothing to lose

A lonely bed, salt spread across the room

Called upon death with no reason to resume

Shadows behind my back, chasing blood perfume

Stiff I chose to lay, covered by my gloom

CONFESSION

Death,

I see glamour in your arms

Beaded with jewels, necklaces and rage

Such a seductress with your charms

Golden beauty, past the anger, no age

Death,

What made you lose all hopes in life

Were you trapped inside a cage?

And if you truly are a happy wife

Why act like a broken widow onstage?

But Death,

I've been meaning to tell

I know you're just a little girl,

despite heaven and hell

And I don't know if it's me

that fascinates you

Or you that fascinates me

But I've fallen for you

Your thought keeps me happy

11:11

No one believes me but I've seen heaven

My dad wanted to see me before I turned seven

Seven in the morning

This special summer day

Everyone was in mourning

But you still found a way

Just a tiny girl of four

A girl genuinely so pure

Cursed by the fact that she could see you no more

You told me you were proud as you walked away

My little-self reassured you that she'd be okay

I watched you grow old in a matter of seconds

Not many can say that their fathers rest in heaven

CAN I CRY TO COMMEMORATE?

Bathing in the fountain of tears

of all the heavenly souls

Acting deaf to the shrieking

down those hollow holes

And I'm sorry that I'm blind

And that I cannot see

Is it all that remains of you?

Or is it all that remains of me?

Been wandering in a place

Out in the outer space

Been chanting some words

Just the adverse case

It's intensified but it sounds so mundane

Have I been morphed or am I that far away?

Can I cry to commemorate?

And to everything that's left

I can only say-

I'd ask you to be nice

And to open your mind wide

Trust me, I've tried

Never works to hide

MELANCHOLIA

He told me to get a taste of drowning to know what's life

Defeat is the catalyst in the process to rise

But in moments like these, no breath suffice

In moments like these, not a tear in my eye

It's dry

It's dry

It's dry

My body, his soul, my mind

There's no water to bring back the life

Not enough to even make me want to die

Consumed by horror, the apple of my eye

And he's terrified

I'm scared, I might lose my only guy

I'm scared, I might never see that tattoo on his left thigh

There seems no end to this eclipse,

it's almost night-time

No sunrise, just salt lime

And the fabricated fact that I'll be fine

FOREVER IS A HAPPY LIE

I watched a lady scream- "dude why?"

With a slight undertone of a cry

As she laid beside her dead old guy

How to mould the truth to their daughter?

How will she even lie?

She's trying to wipe up each eye

Her little girl goes-"mama please don't cry"

We all know that forever is a happy lie

That's what her father always taught her

But her question remains-why?

NEVER TO LOOK BACK

I've been wasting time

like bees on honey

Hoping one day

you'll finally want me

But it's kinda funny

You're kinda funny

So funny

It goes beyond me

I went past the line

crossed that extra mile

Never to look back

and I can't,

Can't imagine us face to face

Crying, as you rest your case

Painted each shade

except for grace

Cried, for it all to fade

And I lied

I never needed space

Drew hopes out of

Altered memories

Wrote songs with

Stolen melodies

There's no way for me

To come back

Home's too far away

CHILD'S CRY

Father, tell me

How to undo this damage that was

done upon me

Right after they disconnected me

from an umbilical cord

Drank potion of tears

from playtime bruises

I counted years,

but misunderstood their uses

Inflicting fears,

those ugly beasts that life chooses

Father, tell me

What made your wife hate me?

Can I stay with you,

I won't touch a thing

Or say a word,

unless you ask of me

I know you haven't aged,

but I've grown older

Not trying to seem rude

but maybe a bit bolder

Should I rid mother with this

stain on her shoulder?

Father, be honest

Would you have ever loved me?

I don't seem to recall you,

you're nothing but lost memory

Would you have held my hand

even in moments of your misery

Would I have made you laugh

well, that I don't expect of me

Dad, come mark your absentee

DYBBUK IN A FOREIGN BODY

I'm a dybbuk in a body that doesn't feel mine

Not a human who believes he can outrun time

I'm a sceptic and devotee combined

Bloody pictures for a deadly rewind

So this body doesn't decode a way to resign

Terror stares my mirrored gaze

A stuck-up lover inside a maze

I get lonely sometimes, this shadow won't feel mine

I'm not a satanist, although that's not a crime

Conjured your soul yet I couldn't find

What kept haunting this place or time

Is it your death or by Almighty's design?

So I creep in the dark, where this body lays

Because humanity, it no longer stays

Here or anywhere else

I'm no longer myself

POSEY GUY

His insolence was exceptional

Nothing compared to that fearless smile

One might easily get intimidated by his endearing lies

Although, his complacency was intentional

No other could appear that versatile

But the truth is, he was nothing more than a Posey guy

DARK MIND VALLEY DIVER

I manage to keep my head up higher

Not pretend my love is heavily heightened

But whenever I think I can mature up

I do something briefly blighted

In the dark mind valley, I'm a diver

I don't know why everyone is frightened?

Adding Whitney vodka in my teacup

I come out so short sighted

You see, I've always been a survivor

Of unrequited love that gets u enlightened

Although, I can't really speak up

Rest I'm delusionly delighted

DAY LATE AND A DOLLAR SHORT

Wish to undo the wasteful thought

Before I take it in and vaguely snort

It makes me insane, I feel kinda hot

Because I'm a day late and a dollar short

Wish I could rewind or teleport

Pack my luggage, fake a passport

A wild goose chase, a rotting fort

But I'm a day late and a dollar short

CHARRED REMAINS

Aghast flame dancing on the wick

Virgin white wax molten at its feet

The wind tames, his cipher lover

He blows-

"love no other"

Aghast flame dancing for the wick

I burn him, yet he's foolishly sweet

So blind to my scarlett letter

If I leave,

All for better

Aghast flame dancing on the wick

He pleads, but I'm done with this heat

I will flee, I will finally be free

For the wind, I'll be

Down on my knee

Aghast flame's not dancing for the wick

Deserted her promised lover for a cheat

Shedding blood over breezing lies

Moment she leaves,

Only the wick survives.

IN-BETWEEN PAGES

An ugly handwritten letter

Stuck on page 30, dull old book

It was torn

Held by tape

Addressed to no one knows who

"Remember to be a go-getter

Never get attached to a faithless crook

You were born

To be great

Make people want to look up to you"

He was proud, never better

Found another- 71, that same book

It was to mourn

And undrape

The misanthropist clearly hurt by a few

"I remember telling you to go get her

I made you breakfast and I was shook

You'd sworn

I said I'll wait

Now you're gone, all I ever had was you"

He died for her to lose life, ends letter

Gone, like his father, an unnatural look

And to mourn

A dead shape

Wasn't something I should've looked into

DRIVE

We stop by to shop for candies and cigrettes

You wait for me to tell you to drive; hoping I'll say the words-

Yes! I want to run away with you.

Yes! We can do what true lovers do.

But I look at you and you smile and I smile right back at you

You seem happy

As if it's something you already knew

I feel something only a man diving into the sea would feel, he'd be
terrified while his heart would freestyle the beats

I can't swim but the idea amazes me & I've dreamt about it all my
life

I've dreamt about it since I was a child

And with you, it doesn't seem terrifying

It's so strange, almost as if I'd miss my old life

As if I had one

As if I'll never die

As if something would be left to leave behind

But I look into your eyes, just as you turn to drive

You manage to grace my presence and prove that you'll never forget my essence

You're scared of loving somebody else too

You don't want us to grow apart like those other lovers do

But right now, we bought candies & a pack of cigrettes, and even though it was never said

I've adjusted myself to decipher those thoughts inside your head

But let's keep this thought aside, like we always do

I think

I think I'm in love with you

Because if you ask of me, I'll run a hundred mile

Because if the world ends, I'll look for you and smile

ONLY MORONS REEK OF LOVE

3 a.m. company, late late-night

Heartful welcome, pale moonlight

Morning strikes in golden lines

Serenade me till the sun shines

Rosey bushes but your thorny eyes

Letting me in, on your private lies

Maybe you're pretty, loyalty aside

Maybe I love you, but at what price?

Betrayal in your blood, philandering your type

Ice cold heart but that warm touch your hype

I know I shouldn't love you but I'll forget by night

In love, they say "nothing's wrong, nothing right"

But "Is the world strange or our love vile?"

Only if I could erase your engraved smile

Comes another day, we roll the same dice

I know I love you, but at what price?

Sweet all summer, by autumn we fight

Dumb and dumber, no string to our kite

Kept you close, but could never rely

So it goes, fall from that great high

Your faithless love, so empty, so vague

Heavy on ego, our heart's plague

Painting the pain in all shades of grey

So maybe I'll let go

But maybe another day

DON'T FALL FOR A GYPSY HEART

I opened my chest for you,

so you could touch a dancing heart

Maybe if you see it, you'd believe it really exists

Little did I know,

you kept a jar of stolen hearts

and traded them for sadness dressed in red

I'm sure that you'll change and that I'd be dead

if i don't run and just lay here instead

But tonight,

I'll steal my stolen heart

I'll sprint till my dying breath.

ACHE OF LONGING

I set the door of longing on fire

A burning room I'd never enter again

Today, I stand here

In the lobby,

over the ashes

The door burnt and the room is open again

LEMONADE

I touched the handle

of the doorway

to your bedroom

You're burning,

like a candle

filled with dust

and lust fumes

You call me "lemonade"

You lay eyes

as if to consume me

Not- ready,

unsteady

I feel like a baby

You're burning

You can take a sip

Maybe?

Convince me with your serenade

Do you think I'm sweet?

or sour?

or atleast tasty?

I take in your heat

yet, you seem far

It's so hasty

I'm coming off shy

I'm scared

You'd say goodbye

But I'm your "lemonade"

SEMI-PSYCHOPATH

It's an old habit of mine, to always look behind
That's what I always did, whenever a lover left me
I stumbled on my path, just so I could fall into your wrath

I will always be nice, even when you're extremely unkind
That's who I really am, even though my sanity has left me
I bathe in this regret, you really made me a semi psychopath

WHEN TOMORROW COMES

Tomorrow

When you wake up

I'll serve you a cup of coffee

And you'll serve me a cup

Of tears

I'll drink it with delight

You give no choice to drown

Now I know

You'll be leaving soon

I'll drink coffee when I cry

That coffee

Will mimic you

Tomorrow

When it's time

I'll pack your clothes

So happily,

I'll watch you go

I'll catch you around

Say you'll stay

near

I'll look for the moon

In our starless sky

That moon too

Will mimic you

Tomorrow

I will write

How I was so terrified

The night before

I started it with a

Simple Hi

Today's chapter is

Give a good-bye

End it with an almost

Happy smile

Tomorrow is the day

I let go

HEAVEN-MADE

I am just a naive girl writing dumb poetry
They told me age wasn't just a number
I could, in fact, sense myself fade

I was never meant to be a timeless beauty
Or long-lastingly stiff like lumber
But somehow, I felt heaven made

SLOW, LET GO

Breathing in briskly

Still, my body, stiff

Watching my breath go by

Shallow as days gone by

Coloured the air grey

And somewhat white

Unafraid what might take my life

Shutting these windows

Some call 'eyes'

It's more lucid

To ones who are somewhat blind

If you can't see, don't see

Just feel the sun strike your eye

You're nimble

So nicely numb

"Don't cry, go bite your thumb"

Smell the smoke

Slow,

let go

Now you're relieved

SICKNESS IS SOLACE

On our beloved Earth,

When the first witch was born

Ever since that birth,

No spells were to be sworn

Indestructible, is what the mortals knew

Inescapable luck, as suggested by the few

Years passed, under the witch's aid

Tribes that came, gradually forgotten away

Lonely she stood, lonely she prayed

Painted sky blue and some white-ish grey

Immortality's hex was such a wonderful sin

She disguised her elixir, beneath a wolf's skin

Laid lifeless by the bed in some lonesome room

Her departure then marked "the origin of doom"

Myriad of kings sprinted but fell to dust

Mightiest of mighty, proud rulers of earth

Castles were stacked, to be engulfed by rust

Lives upon lives drowned in power's worth

Those Ruins laid trampled below soldiers feet

Who bid several lifetimes, but to their defeat

They wanted a world with equity and peace

But the world they borrowed was lent on lease

To their dismay, corpses are buried in dirt

Dead kings & soldiers, all wearing the same shirt

Blood on whose hands, graves are dug

Death meant doom or food to some bug?

The King yearned power, soldiers rebel reign

Then came a poet, philosophy somewhat sane

You can wield power, gain vigour and fame

But to love is to flourish, beyond such bane

But those lovers left, like those lovers came

Till his soul shattered, received presents of pain

Upon perishing, his words washed down by rain

Are we flourishing or is it the witch's mistake?

She resorted to death, for what sake?

Will there come a God to undo this mistake?

But is that decision hers or ours to take?

I suppose sickness is solace, a second breath

When I succumb to life, I succumb to death

If we watch closely, let doom shed its skin

The witch left something, within people akin

Beyond the ravages of time, an ephemeral plan

Sickness brought hope to the last dying man

The society was sick, the bygones are gone

To flourish isn't to win a gamble enthralling pawns

When the witch is back,

Will our fears attack?

Maybe the world will thrive upon colouring it black.

RUINS

Holy

And unholy

Pleasant and pleased

Alive but dead

Dead but not deceased

My world wasn't substantial

Yet You denigrated my disease

God,

Aren't You as guilty as me?

When, in ashes, I laid burnt

Was that a lesson to-be learnt?

Shot down in a wild hunt

Was it real or just a stunt?

Now I turn those crumbling wheels

Is this how impotency really feels?

I ruined myself, and You let me

God,

You made me my worst enemy

HEY ANGER!

I talked to a stranger

Whom I referred to as
"anger"
I felt a connection
buried beneath
My heart was pouring
amber
On the fancy table
A candle was lit
Her calm mid-night
glamour
all designer fit
I joked about my
dirty rugby t-shirt
washed stains
That's it
No, I never bother
I even said, "the dinner
tastes like shit"
Soon, the wax melted

slowly,

the Sun rose up
Out, at a distance
I could finally see her
bright
and much clearer
Reflecting all the light
all that ever came
near her
She still seemed calm
almost Godly, a bit
I called for her
"anger"
She corrected,
her name was
'grief'

9 798889 868163

Printed by Libri Plureos GmbH in Hamburg,
Germany